Get the Mes...

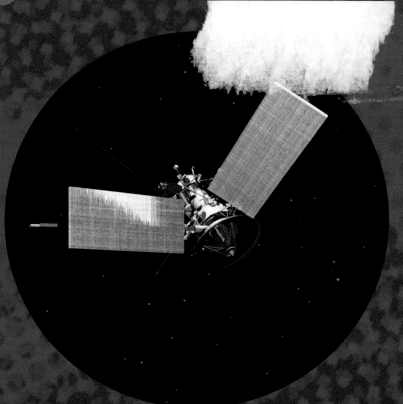

Written by Haydn Middleton
Adapted by Jackie Holderness
for the Heinemann English Readers series

Heinemann

Heinemann Educational Publishers
Halley Court, Jordan Hill, Oxford OX2 8EJ

An imprint of Harcourt Education Limited
Heinemann is a registered trademark of Harcourt Education Limited.

© Haydn Middleton 2006

10 09 08 07 06
10 9 8 7 6 5 4 3 2 1

British Library Cataloguing in Publication Data is available from the British Library on request.

ISBN 0435 294512 / 978 0435 294519

Designed by Nicola Kenwood @ Hakoona Matata Designs
Illustrated by Moreno Chiacchiera, Andy Peters, Andy Parker and Ned Jolliffe

Cover design by Nicola Kenwood @ Hakoona Matata Designs
Cover photograph reproduced with permission of Harcourt Education Ltd/Rob Judges

Printed and bound in Malaysia by Vivar

Acknowledgements
The publishers would like to thank the following for permission to reproduce photographs: Getty
Images/PhotoDisc p.6; Getty Images/PhotoDisc p.7 (top); Harcourt Education Ltd/Tudor Photography
p.7 (bottom); Getty Images/PhotoDisc p.8 (left); Corbis p.8 (right); Science Photo Library p.9 (top); Getty
Images/PhotoDisc p.9 (bottom); Superstock p.13; photos.com p.18; Corbis p.19

Every effort has been made to contact copyright holders of material reproduced in this book. Any
omissions will be rectified in subsequent printings if notice is given to the publishers.

Get the Message

Contents

Some words in this book are bold, **like this**.
You can find these words in the glossary.

signal

message

HELP

body language

traffic light

advertisement

road sign

DRINK ORANGE JUICE!

screen email

satellite

computer

text message

mobile phone

emoticon   hieroglyphs   morse code

ARE YOU GETTING THE MESSAGE?

When we meet people, we talk to them. We tell jokes, ask questions and swap news. Talking is a good way of **communicating**. Even when we can't meet, we can still communicate with each other. We do it by sending messages.

to get the message: to understand
to swap: to exchange

Sharing secrets

When you talk to a friend, you can share secrets by whispering. In messages you can share secrets by using **codes** that only you and your friend will understand.

Using our eyes and ears

For some messages we need to use our eyes, like when we read an email. For other messages we need to use our ears, like when we answer the phone.

Sounds and signals

We do not have to use words to communicate. We can also make sounds. We can blow a whistle. We can clap our hands. Or we can give **signals**. This book describes many different ways of sending messages. It also gives ideas for some clever ways to send secret messages to your friends!

to whisper: to talk very quietly
like when: such as when, for example when

MESSAGES BY MOBILE

Lots of people use mobile phones to send messages. Mobiles are very useful in emergencies, for example, when a car breaks down. If you are a long way from a public telephone, you can still ring for help. People also use mobiles just to chat.

Hey Andrew! Guess where I am!

Help!

Small is beautiful

Telephones have been around since 1876. Mobile phones came many years later.

The first mobile phones were big and heavy.

This modern mobile phone is easy to carry and use.

to break down: to stop working
to chat: to talk with people you know well
since 1876: from 1876 onwards

How mobiles work

Mobile phones are in fact small radios.
They send the sound of your voice to a **base station** nearby.
Then the base station **transmits** the sound to your friend's phone.

When you talk into a phone, the phone turns the sound into electrical signals. When the signals reach your friend's phone, they turn back into sound.

Hello!

This is a base station. It transmits sounds from one phone to another.

Hello!

Satellites in outer space can also be used to send phone signals.

's (apostrophe of possession)
This is my friend's mobile.
The man listened to the lady's voice.

Text messages

Sometimes you or your friend can't talk on the phone. You can still send a text message from your mobile phone to your friend's mobile. Your friend can read it and reply later.

IGd2Txt

Texting is a quick, fun way of sending a message. You can use these shorter ways of typing some words:

@ – at
B – be
CN – seeing
4 – for
GR8 – great
Hv – have
IGd2Tlk – it's good to talk

JK – just kidding
L8R – later
LOKn – looking
LOL – lots of love OR
      I'm laughing out
      loud
Mob – mobile phone
N2MU – nice to meet you
R – are
SWALK – sealed with
        a loving kiss
U – you
Wht – what
Zzz – I'm tired

Emoticons

Emoticons are little faces that show how you feel about someone or something. You can add them to text messages or emails.
You have to look at them sideways!

:-)   happy   :-(sad face   :-O   surprised

:-S   unsure   :-P   cheeky

What do these messages mean?

:-))))Xmas   U Mke Me :-)

to reply: to answer

10

DO YOU WANT TO HEAR A SECRET?

You need to say something private to a friend, but other people are in the room. What can you do? You can talk in code.

Loony Latin

Loony Latin is a good code to use when you are talking. This is how you put normal words into Loony Latin.

If a word begins with a **vowel**, just add 'ay' to the end of it. Here's the name 'Andrew' in Loony Latin:

Andreway

If a word begins with a **consonant**, move the first letter to the end of the word. So the name 'Jade' becomes 'Adej'.

Jade   Adej

Then add 'ay' to it:

Adejay

See if you can work out what this secret Loony Latin message means:

Ouryay   Rouserstay   Areay   Onay   Ackbay

Otay   Rontfay.

(Clue – start by taking the 'ay' off all the words.)

It takes a lot of practice to talk fast in Loony Latin!

---

loony: crazy
practice (noun) / practise (verb)
My Loony Latin needs lots of practice. I need to practise every day.

CONTACT BY COMPUTER

Letters can take a long time to arrive. Phone calls can be expensive. A quick, cheap way to communicate is by email. (The 'e' stands for 'electronic'.) Most emails are quite short messages.

Follow the email trail

Here's how an email travels from one computer to another.

1 Andrew types an email on his computer. Now he can send it to Jade's email address over the **Internet**.

2 The email travels along a telephone line to a computer. This computer is Andrew's **mail server**. The mail server reads Jade's email address.

4 The message is stored here until Jade is ready to **download** it to her own computer. Then she can read it.

3 Then Andrew's mail server sends his email along another telephone line to Jade's mail server.

Jade can be in the next room or a thousand miles away. The message from Andrew still takes just a few seconds to arrive.

12

opposites
cheap / expensive   short / long   near / far

A computer from the 1970s.

The first email was sent in 1971 by an engineer called Ray Tomlinson. Computers in the 1970s looked very different from the way they look now!

Instant messaging

If you go **online** at the same time as several friends, you can use an instant messaging **program**. As soon as you send a message, it appears on all your friends' screens.

You can use your own special nickname instead of your real name if you like. On the screen below is a conversation between three friends. They have used funny nicknames!

Address: @ messaging program

Robot boy says: What are you doing this Saturday?

Sunshine says: My grandparents are coming.

Geek says: I'm going to see Manchester United play.

Robot boy says: I don't believe you! No one can get tickets for Manchester United games.

Sunshine says: No, he is going. His dad knows the manager.

Robot boy says: You're soooooooo lucky! Can I come too? Pleeeeeease?

But be careful! Never talk to strangers when you're online and never give your name and address.

different from
Old computers looked different from modern ones.
Jade's mobile phone is different from Andrew's.

Business or pleasure?

Some emails have to be written in a formal, serious way. But emails to friends can be very informal, like text messages on a mobile. The same person wrote both the emails below.

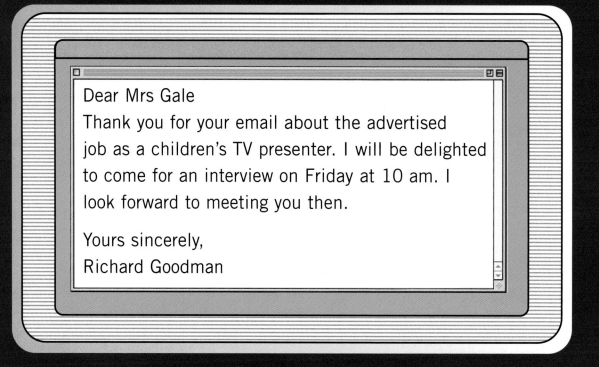

Dear Mrs Gale
Thank you for your email about the advertised job as a children's TV presenter. I will be delighted to come for an interview on Friday at 10 am. I look forward to meeting you then.

Yours sincerely,
Richard Goodman

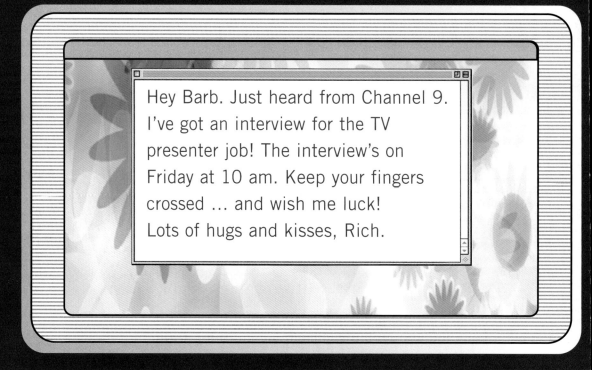

Hey Barb. Just heard from Channel 9. I've got an interview for the TV presenter job! The interview's on Friday at 10 am. Keep your fingers crossed ... and wish me luck!
Lots of hugs and kisses, Rich.

opposites
formal / informal
delighted / disappointed

DO YOU WANT TO READ A SECRET?

Sometimes you might need to send a secret message to a friend. In wartime people often send written messages containing important information. These messages need to be in code so that the enemy cannot read them.

Hiding the meaning

Julius Caesar had a good way of fooling his enemies. When Caesar wrote a message, he jumbled up the letters. For example, instead of writing 'a', he could write 'd', which comes three letters after 'a'. Instead of 'b', he could write 'e' – and so on through the alphabet. This is called using a **cipher**.

CIPHER ALPHABET

D E F G H I J K L M N O P Q R S T U V W X Y Z A B C

a b c d e f g h i j k l m n o p q r s t u v w x y z

REAL ALPHABET

Only Caesar's friends and **allies** would know how he jumbled the letters. And since they understood his cipher, they could easily read the message. But to an enemy it made no sense at all.

Can you decipher this message that Caesar might have sent?

QR ILJKWLQJ WRGDB. PB VROGLHUV KDYH WXPPB-DFKH.

---

conditional tense
will / would   can / could   may / might
to jumble up: to mix things together

Hiding the message

Histaiaeus, an ancient Greek, once shaved off a messenger's hair, wrote a message on his bald head, then waited for the messenger's hair to grow back. The messenger travelled safely past the enemy. Then he shaved his head again that an ally could read the message.

Message in a microdot

In World War Two, German spies wrote a top-secret message and photographed it. Then they shrank the photograph until it became a tiny dot called a microdot. Finally they wrote an ordinary letter, hid the dot on top of one of the full stops, and sent it home to Germany. If enemies got hold of the letter, they would find no useful information in it. But when it reached Germany, people there could **magnify** the dot and read the secret message.

irregular past tenses
write / wrote   shrink / shrank   hide / hid   send / sent   get / got
to shrink: to make something smaller

Shhhh!

Build your own cipher alphabet

Ciphers are sometimes based on a key word. You can use your own name for this.

> First, take out any repeated letters, e.g. SARAH would become SARH.

After the last letter in your name, put all the other letters of the alphabet, in their normal order. Remember not to include the letters of your name twice! When you reach Z, start again at the beginning of the alphabet so that you have used every letter once.

> S A R H I J K L M N O P Q T U V W X Y Z B C D E F G

Finally match up each letter with the letters in the real alphabet:

CIPHER ALPHABET
S A R H I J K L M N O P Q T U V W X Y Z B C D E F G
↓ ↓
a b c d e f g h i j k l m n o p q r s t u v w x y z
REAL ALPHABET

What does the message RUQI WBMROPF mean, using this cipher?

Write a cipher question to someone using your own name as the key word. They must answer using a cipher based on their name.

once: one time
twice: two times

MESSAGES WITHOUT WORDS

We send many messages without using words. In fact most of our communication is done through looks and **gestures**. We understand each other's body language, so there is often no need to talk.

Getting the picture

We can tell what jobs nurses or footballers do just by looking at their uniforms. We know it is safe to cross a busy road when we see the sign of a little green man. In each case, we understand the **visual** message that we are seeing.

Drivers have to know what road signs mean. This sign means 'People working on the road ahead'.

body language: the meanings we understand from gestures and body positions such as smiling, waving and so on
uniform: special clothing worn by someone for their job or school

Misleading messages

I love spiders.

People's body language can give a different message from the words they speak. A person might say, 'I'm feeling very brave!' But if he is twitching and sweating, you know he is really very nervous.

Wordless writing

Today we know how to read the picture-writing of the ancient Egyptians - knows as **hieroglyphics**. Experts learned how to read hieroglyphics around the year 1800. Until then, no one could understand these wordless messages from thousands of years ago.

Some of the pictures, known as **ideograms**, show the things being described. Others stand for sounds, like the letters in our own alphabet.

We use only 26 letters. Egyptian writers used about 700 different ideograms!

Reading the signals

Sometimes we urgently need to send messages without words. In an emergency, sailors at sea contact other ships by using flags. This one – known as 'Victor' – means that the ship needs help.

This ship needs help!

Sailors all over the world learn the meanings of signals like this. Then, whatever languages they speak, they will understand what they see.

to nod: to move your head up and down
to twitch: to shake nervously
to sweat: to produce a liquid out of your skin when you are hot or uncomfortable

Semaphore

Semaphore is an old way of transmitting messages between high places that are far apart. By holding out your arms in these positions – with or without flags – you can show a sequence of letters. These build up into words, and then into a message.

Around the year 1800 in France, people used telescopes to read semaphore messages from as far as 16 km away. By 1846, there were 534 semaphore stations all over France. Messages sent between them could travel quickly from one end of France to the other.

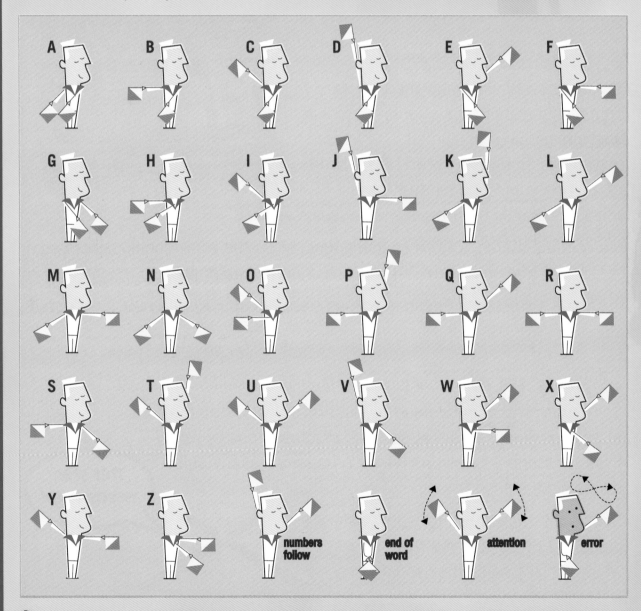

opposites
quickly / slowly   with / without
high / low   far apart / near

MESSAGES BY MORSE

Well, either there's an army on the way, or the toast is burning!

Sending a message over a long distance is called telegraphy. In ancient times people did this by transmitting smoke, fire or drum signals. Then, in the 1840s, people found a way of communicating over much longer distances – by using electrical telegraphy.

Sending an electric telegraph message

In the 1800s, people sent telegraph messages in Morse code. First the sender tapped on a little lever. The lever sent bursts of electrical **current** along a wire. Some of the bursts were short and some were long.

Then, at the other end of the wire, the bursts came out on a roll of paper as a **sequence** of dots and dashes.

the sender

the receiver

Finally, the receiver read the message. Each dot and each dash stood for letters, numbers and punctuation marks (see p. 22). This telegraph language was called Morse code. Morse messages could travel along wires that ran for many miles underneath the land or sea.

lever: the part of a machine that you push to make it work
burst: a sudden increase in something for a short moment

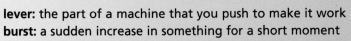

Here are all the letters of the alphabet in international Morse code.

A	•—	H	••••	O	———	V	•••—
B	—•••	I	••	P	•——•	W	•——
C	—•—•	J	•———	Q	——•—	X	—••—
D	—••	K	—•—	R	•—•	Y	—•——
E	•	L	•—••	S	•••	Z	——••
F	••—•	M	——	T	—		
G	——•	N	—•	U	••—		

Can you read this Morse question?
(...and answer it in Morse code too?)

•——/••••/•—/—/   ••/•••/   —•—/———/•••/•—•/   •••—/••—/•—••/•—••/   —•/•—/——/•/?

The 'slashes' (/) show you where each letter ends.

The man who invented Morse code was the American artist, Samuel F. B. Morse (1791–1872). His first telegraph line was completed in 1844, from Baltimore to Washington in the USA.

dates in words
1791 = seventeen hundred and ninety-one
1872 = eighteen hundred and seventy-two

The word 'telegraphy' was first used in English in about 1792. It comes from the Greek words for 'far' (tele) and 'to write' (graphein). What do you think the words 'telephone', 'telecommunications' and 'television' actually mean?

Sending a message in the dark

In emergencies – especially when it is dark – people still use Morse code. They send sound bleeps on a radio, or flashes of light from a lamp or torch. Instead of dot / dash, you use long-bleep / short-bleep, or long-flash / short-flash.

You could use a torch to send a Morse code message to a friend in the dark.

You could use ...
You could use a torch to send a message.
You could use a mobile phone to call for help.

Can you read this text message?

Hv U Fnd Wht U R LOKn 4?

Use the information on p.10 to help you.

What does this message in the Caesar cipher say?

LI BRX GRQ'W OLNH WKH PHVVDJH,
GRQ'W VKRRW WKH PHVVHQJHU.

Use the information on p.15 to help you.

Can you decipher this message in semaphore?

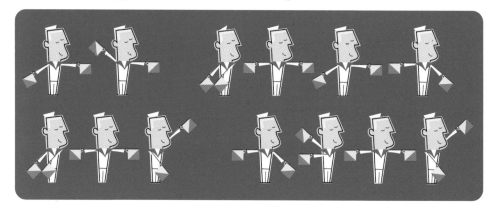

Use the information on p.20 to help you.

Answer these questions about the text in full sentences. (In some of the activities that follow, the first question has been done to help you.)

1 How do we communicate with each other? *We communicate with each other by talking and by sending messages.*

2 How have mobile phones changed?

3 Who sent the first email and when?

4 Which job did Richard Goodman want?

5 When was his interview with Mrs Gale?

6 Which Roman Emperor jumbled up letters to make a cipher alphabet?

7 Which country used microdots in the war?

8 When did people first learn how to decipher Egyptian hieroglyphs?

9 What did some people use to read semaphore messages?

10 Samuel Morse invented Morse code. What else did he do?

1 Match the nickname to the people here:

1 Skinny Minnie   2 George the Giraffe
3 Speedy   4 Princess
5 Leo the Lion   6 Spots

2 Write Barb's reply to Rich (see p.14). What would she say? You could try using some of the emoticons on p.10 in your reply.

3 Write a message to a friend in Morse code.

4 Check each of the glossary words in a dictionary. Are the definitions the same? Which is easier to understand? Use each glossary word in sentences of your own.

Read the phrases below. Fill in the missing words with the -ing form of the verb shown in brackets.

1 Are you … the message? (get) *(Are you getting the message?)*

2 … secrets (share)

3 … our eyes and ears (use)

4 … the meaning (hide)

5 … the message (receive)

6 … the picture (get)

7 … the signals (read)

8 … an email (send)

What do you notice when you add -ing to a word? How does it change the spelling?

Find five more -ing words in the book. Use these -ing words and try to make up five new sentences of your own.

Fill in the missing letters in each computer screen, so that the sentences make sense.

1

W... are you going this Friday? What are you ... this Saturday?

On Friday I'm ... to the cinema. On Saturday, I... having my birthday party.

2

W...'s coming to your ...?

My aunt and u... are coming. My grand... are coming. The whole family is ...!

3

And what are you doing this S..., Spiderman?

I'm ... to see a football match. I'm ... Manchester United ...

4

But it's very difficult to get ... for their games.

But Spiderman's dad ... the manager so he can get the tickets.

5

Can I come to the football ... too?

No, I'm sorry. I can only ... two tickets.

6

Never mind, you can ... to my party!

Here are some questions. Answer each one in a full sentence.

1 Can you count how many pages there are in *Get the Message*? *Yes, I can. There are 32 pages.*

2 Can you communicate without using your voice?

3 Can you remember when the first telephone appeared?

4 Can you send a text message?

5 Can you find a picture of an early computer?

6 Can you explain what 'to magnify' means?

7 Can you describe the Egyptian picture on p.19?

8 Can you write your name in Morse code?

9 Can you work out for how long Samuel Morse lived?

Background

1 Let the students write text message letters, using texting techniques on paper!

2 Make a display of road signs, labelled in English.

3 Give the students some string and two empty yoghurt pots. Show them how to make a simple phone by putting a hole in the bottom of each pot and tying each end of the string through each hole. One child can speak into one pot whilst another child holds the other pot against his or her ear.

4 Encourage the students to make email friends with children in an English-speaking country. Try an e-pals website or make contact with a UK or US school, or one in New Zealand, Eire, Australia or South Africa. Make sure you get parents' permission first!

5 Encourage the students to find out more about satellites: how they work, who puts them into space and maintains them etc.

How to get the most out of this book

1 It is helpful if the students can read the book in pairs, reading one page aloud each. Reading aloud should help with recall and it also encourages the students' application of words and phrases.

2 Encourage the students to look at the key words pages before reading the rest of the book. These pages are designed to be used as a picture glossary. It is also helpful to have an English dictionary available for the students to use.

3 The coloured strips at the bottom of each page show the language used in the text in either a different way or a different context, or may help introduce a new word. Looking at these will help the students to better understand the text and to develop their English.

Answers

Try it yourself!
1 b
2 f
3 a
4 d
5 c
6 e

Adding -ing
1 getting
2 sharing
3 using
4 hiding
5 receiving
6 getting
7 reading
8 sending

An online conversation!
1 Where/doing/going/am
2 Who's/party/uncle/grandparents/coming
3 Saturday/going/watching/play
4 tickets/is
5 match/get
6 come

Read and remember
1 We communicate with each other by talking and by sending messages.
2 Mobile phones have got smaller and lighter and are easier to use.
3 The first email was sent in 1971 by Ray Tomlinson.
4 Richard Goodman wanted the job as a children's TV presenter.
5 His interview with Mrs Gale was on Friday at 10 am.
6 Julius Caesar jumbled up letters to make a cipher alphabet.
7 Germany used microdots in the war.
8 People first learnt how to decipher Egyptian hieroglyphs around the year 1800.
9 Some people used telescopes to read semaphore messages.
10 Samuel Morse was also an artist.

Now try these
1 Have you found what you are looking for?
2 If you don't like the message don't shoot the messenger.
3 My arms are sore.

Glossary

allies	people fighting for the same side in a war
attachments	**files** sent as part of an email
base station	a place that picks up and sends out mobile phone **signals**
cipher	a secret way of writing
codes	ways of hiding the meaning of messages
to communicate	to make contact with people
consonant	any alphabet letter which is not a, e, i, o, or u
current	the movement of electricity
to decipher	to work out the meaning of
to download	to transfer information to a computer
files	containers of computer information
gestures	movements of parts of the body that can express a meaning
hieroglyphics	an ancient kind of writing using picture-symbols
ideogram	a written sign or symbol used in some writing systems, which describes an idea or object
Internet	a system of computers all over the world, linked together by telephone lines
to magnify	to make bigger
mail server	a kind of email post office
online	connected to the **Internet**
program	instructions given to a computer to make it do things
sequence	a set of things arranged in order
signals	signs or objects which give a message
to transmit	to send electronically
visual	to do with seeing
vowel	the alphabet letters a, e, i, o, and u

Index